Gambling Addiction Cure

How to Overcome Gambling Addiction and Stop Compulsive Gambling For Life

Anthony Wilkenson

Legal Disclaimer

Introduction

Is gambling an innocent past time? Is it a way to fund education or something that helps our community, something you can do for extra income? Is it merely a recreation activity?

There are 3 basic elements of gambling

1. There is an uncertain arbitrary event

2. There is the wager (something of value) that is deliberately   chanced on a particular outcome

3. There is a winner and a loser - The winner wins at the direct loss of the other gambler(s)

Whether your addiction involves betting your hard-earned money on sports, roulette, slots, poker or scratch cards in casinos both online and offline, you are about to discover an effective and proven strategy to overcome gambling addiction. Gambling addiction, when left uncured, can strain or damage your relationships with your family and friends, interfere with your productivity and work schedules, and may cause you to deal with a financial crisis in the long run.

Do not wait for your addiction to cause you to do things that you never thought you are capable of doing. Millions of people who suffer from gambling addiction engage in destructive behavior that is uncontrollable. They lie, cheat, steal from their own family just to keep the action going. These compulsive gamblers won't stop until their life is ruined.

But don't think that there is no hope for you. You might think that you can no longer stop this addiction, but be aware that with the right kind of help, it is possible to get rid of this addiction and finally regain full control of your life.

With your determination and discipline, you will finally be able to get rid of your gambling addiction and protect yourself and your loved ones from financial disaster. All it takes is for you to recognize and acknowledge that you have the problem, read, and apply the principles outlined in this book, and you will conquer gambling addiction for good.

This book will help you understand what gambling addiction is and how you can overcome this horrible addiction. By grabbing a copy of this book, you have increased your chances of achieving full recovery. You will also learn how to get the right support when it comes to making positive financial choices.

- *An overview of gambling addiction*

  This section will talk about the basics of the condition, provide a simple explanation as to why many people find it difficult to get over it, and dispel some of the common misconceptions surrounding gambling addiction. Additionally, you can do some self-diagnosis by looking at our gambling addiction checklist.

- *Psychological treatments for gambling addiction*

  Want to know which treatments will work for gambling addicts? We'll enumerate these methods and a simple explanation as to the concepts applied by each therapy method.

- *Self-help methods to cure gambling addiction*

  Not getting results from your therapist? Then you might need to do something as well. This chapter will show you what you need to do to get started on the road to recovery.

- *Utilizing the bond*

  The third wheel that can make recovery faster is the family, especially the spouse. Is the problem present in your husband or wife? Learn how to help him/her overcome the problem with our proven tips.

1: What is gambling addiction?

Addiction takes many forms. Aside from being addicted to sex, drugs and alcohol, another form of addiction that anyone can have is gambling addiction. This chapter will aim to explore what this condition is about.

What is gambling addiction?

Just as the name suggests, gambling addiction or compulsive gambling refers to the condition of being hooked on gambling. Like the other "cousins" of addiction, the person who experiences this problem finds it difficult to control his urge for gambling. This particular behavior is something that the individual engages on consistently regardless of his current situation.

Even if those who suffer from this addiction are on the verge of being broke or even already broke, they just find it too difficult not to bet for "one last time". They know that they are losing and they already know that they are compromising many things just to continue gambling; it's just that they can't stop themselves from betting.

Is it considered an illness?

According to the 4th edition of the Diagnostic and Statistical Manual for Mental Disorders (DSM-IV), gambling addiction (along with other forms of addiction) are considered as mental disorders, grouped under impulse control disorders. Its primary symptom is that the individual finds it very difficult to stop what they're doing even if they know that they should stop. It's similar to a habit – the body moves automatically even though you do not intend to engage in such behavior.

What contributes to this problem?

It is said that one contributor as to why people develop gambling addiction is because the system of gambling itself provides intermittent rewards.

This concept refers to getting something desirable (in this case, winning the amount of money that you and your opponent have betted on the outcome of the game) that isn't continuous. This is always present in gambling.

This is because you cannot ensure that the next rounds of cards and/or betting will be in your favor. You'll never know when you'll experience the good feeling when you win, thus influencing you to continue betting in the hope of experiencing another win. People on the losing side also think the same way. Since they don't know when they will win unless they bet, they continue to gamble.

Your gambling addiction checklist

Worried that you or someone you know is addicted to gambling? The following are some of the signs and symptoms experienced by people with this condition. If you experience the majority of these, then it may be time that you seek professional help.

- You find it hard to walk away from a bet. You think there is nothing wrong to bet on a game. However, if you're finding it difficult to control yourself from placing a bet even if you have already won enough, then this is something that you should be wary of.

- You continue to gamble even if you don't have money. Losing is normal in gambling. But if you're trying desperately to recover your losses by gambling even more, then you have a gambling addiction problem

  This is because people who experience such condition often resort to compromising money that is to be spent on more important things such as tuition fees or mortgage in the hope of winning big and getting back what they lost.

If they are very desperate, they may even engage in extremes such as selling things (or even stealing things that can be sold) or borrowing money. Gambling addicts are oblivious of the fact that if they continue to gamble, they may be making the hole where they are already in larger.

- You are secretive about your gambling activities. People who are addicted to gambling are discreet when it comes to how often they gamble or how much they've lost. In some cases, they may even deny altogether that they are still gambling especially when their family members or friends start to ask.

They believe that these people will not understand them if they divulge their information. It may also be that if the gambling addict wins the jackpot, they want these people to be surprised.

- The gambling disrupts your functioning and encroaches on other areas in your life. This is a common sign of people who experience any kind of addiction. If the addiction causes problems to any sphere in his/her life such as family, school or work and the community (when the person is not able to fulfill the roles expected of him), then he definitely needs some kind of help.

Busting myths about gambling addiction

False beliefs also surround gambling addiction. This section will enumerate what these myths are and bust them by presenting the facts.

People who gamble everyday are gambling addicts

The most common misconception surrounding this condition revolves on the frequency of gambling. It is believed that a person has gambling addiction if he gambles often or every single day. This however, is a myth.

Although the frequency of gambling is a good method to know if one is addicted to gambling, this method is inconclusive. There are people who bet on horse racing or online slots everyday but do not experience problems in any areas in their life.

On the other hand, some people do not spend too much time on gambling yet experience an irresistible urge to bet every round (or even bet some more even if their last dollar was already lost). Remember, addiction is experienced when you find it difficult to control your urge to do whatever that you're addicted to.

If the gambler is not losing money, no gambling problem is present

You may be very rich and can afford to gamble, but it will not exempt you from being considered as a "gambling addict." Regardless of how much money you lost, you still have a gambling problem if you cannot suppress the need to gamble.

Gambling problems do not revolve on money alone. You may not be losing money, but if you are losing friends or breaking relationships with your family members because of the activity, then you are definitely suffering from an addiction.

Helping the gambler with his financial problems can help him recover from the condition

Another obvious myth is the belief that gambling addicts just continue with their gambling because it's the easiest way to recover their losses and pay back what they owe. Thus, they can recover from gambling addiction if all their debts are taken care of. Unfortunately, this is opposite of what will really happen.

If you pay the debt of the addicted gambler, you are unconsciously telling him that he can continue to gamble because you are there to take care of any losses that he will incur. You put him in a position where he can gamble without limit as he will always have a "clean slate" with your help.

Gambling problem is developed because of relationship problems

The long-running attribution of gambling addicts when asked about the possible cause of their addiction is they have problems with their relationships, especially with their family or husband/wife. However, this is a misinterpretation on the part of the gambler.

The real situation could be that their family wants them to stop gambling because of its adverse effects to their finances and relationship. Unfortunately, the gambler thinks that these people do not understand him, turning to gambling as the area that can give him something good (because of the "rewards" that he can gain when he wins).

Now that you have enough knowledge about gambling addiction, the discussion will now proceed to the solutions on how you can help yourself or your loved one to overcome this addiction.

2: Psychological Treatment Option for Gambling Addiction

Seeing that gambling addiction is a psychological disorder, it is also expected that the first solutions that should be employed would be psychological in nature. This chapter will discuss some of the methods that you can use to cure your gambling addiction.

Behavioral therapy methods

Since gambling is a behavioral problem, one of the best therapy methods to employ should be from the behavioral perspective. In behavioral therapy, the focus is to modify what is observable behavior. After all, it is the cause of the problem – not the addicted person's emotions and thoughts.

The following are some of the methods under the behavioral perspective that can be used specifically to help people with gambling addiction:

Daily scheduled activity

A basic behavioral treatment that can be applied to addicted person is to have a daily schedule of activities which should be followed as strictly as possible. It might look like a simple treatment, but it is proven to be effective in controlling the addiction. This is because the following concepts are applied in this treatment:

- When a person is conditioned to be doing a particular activity during a specific time of the day, his body will move automatically to accomplish the task. Rather than think about gambling, his mind will be forced to think of ways on how the task can be done properly.

- When a person's schedule is always full (or almost full), it will be difficult for him to find time when he can gamble. Most gambling addicts are able to engage in gambling because they have too much idle time; this makes gambling the best possible activity that they can use as a substitute for this idle time.

In order to make this treatment more effective, a few practices should also be carried out while the treatment is being applied.

- ***There should be close supervision***

  Humans are prone to cheating and "cutting corners" especially if they have an opportunity. Just because you are the therapist and you assigned them with several tasks that should be accomplished at specific times doesn't mean that they will follow you.

Thus, to ensure that the gambling addict is doing what he is supposed to do at a particular time, you need to closely monitor him. This will force him to comply with what you want him to do. This practice is essentially important especially during the initial phase of the treatment when the person is still struggling to cope with the new practice that he should apply. If the therapist cannot observe the client, then another person should observe the client for him.

- *Providing a performance standard*

  Aside from the supervision, another practice that can make this treatment effective is to provide a standard or quota that the client should be able to reach for each activity by the end of its duration. By doing so, you can be sure that the client is attending to the task and not just doing it for compliance (as it will result in a low quality output).

  If, for example, the person is asked to do the dishes for 30 minutes, there should be a minimum number or quality that he should meet. In this example, you might set the quota of 15 plates and glasses thoroughly rinsed without any grease or food residue.

- Know when to reward and what should be given to him. Once the client is able to accomplish the task given to him, he should be provided with a reward. This is essential so that the behavior that you want him to adapt is repeated. At first, you can provide rewards after he accomplishes the task.

As the response is produced more frequently, you can then give the rewards after a set interval (say, after three days of good performance). The type of reward that is given should be chosen carefully. Never give him a reward that can be used for gambling (such as money or day-off from the scheduled task without your supervision).

Behavioral rehearsal

Another basic therapy method under the behavioral perspective is the behavioral rehearsal. As the name suggests, this method is focused on training individuals to adapt new responses to situations that may be causing the problems.

For gambling addicts, the responses that they should rehearse are related to how they can face situations that may lead them to gamble. The rehearsal can focus on verbal responses (how to say no, how to make excuses when invited to gamble, etc.) as well as behavioral responses (learning to drive away from casinos or other similar places). The idea behind this method is similar to conditioning and forming a habit.

Cognitive behavioral therapy

Also called as rational restructuring, cognitive behavioral therapy (CBT) is a form of counseling method which utilizes the connection between thoughts and behavior to control problems such as those brought by gambling addiction.

The focus of CBT is to identify the individual's thought processes that may be causing him to continue gambling. Once these "irrational" beliefs are determined, the therapist begins to discuss these thoughts and influence the client to change his previous beliefs. By doing so, the client will then be able to control his urge to gamble.

Example:

Gambling addicts think that they are not understood by their family members, and it is only through gambling that they are able to experience the feeling or elation. Therapists can correct this false belief by talking "sense" through them and saying that instead of using gambling to feel happy, they should instead discuss the problems in a person. This continues until the person sees the situation in another light and adapts the more desirable behavior (that is, refraining from gambling).

Group therapy

In layman's term, this refers to support groups. There are many support groups that you can contact to help you with your gambling problem. One popular support group is Gamblers Anonymous.

Group therapies are effective methods because these revolve around cooperation and encouragement. People who are addicted have the belief that "no one understands their predicament". Through the help of support groups that focus on a specific type of addiction, they have the chance to meet other people with the same condition which may help change their previous belief. This will influence clients to cooperate with all the activities in the group, as well as encourage other people that they can overcome the addiction since "they are on the same page". Support groups may also be an avenue where the clients receive "genuine tips" that have been effective to other people in suppressing their urge to engage in this undesirable behavior.

Group therapies are centered on the client's output with the facilitator. They want to be certain that the therapy is followed. Each member of the group is given a chance to speak or share his/her insight regarding the question or situation raised by the facilitator.

The session can also include affirmations (giving another person a hug or positive statement that he can overcome the problem). Group therapies can also foster respect and acceptance to other people, regardless of the severity or background of the member's condition.

It is advised that you look for professionals who have knowledge and experience in administering the treatment methods stated above. This is because, like lawyers, not all therapists are able to provide these methods even if they have an extensive knowledge of psychology.

Just because gambling addicts need the help of a professional does not mean that they are weak. In fact, it takes a lot of courage to admit that they are suffering from this addiction and need help to overcome this problem. It is only when the presence of the condition is recognized that the affected individual become responsive to the therapy methods mentioned above.

3: Self-Help Methods to Cure Gambling Addiction

Aside from psychological treatment methods, the gambling addicts should also help themselves if they want to overcome their addiction. This chapter will discuss some of the self-help methods that can be applied to get rid of gambling addiction.

Start with a reality check

Overcoming your gambling addiction starts with you. The first step is to think about what is happening to you and visualize the consequences if your gambling habit continues. Even if you're outside of your therapy, you should always think of situations such as "What will become of my family if I gamble the money that's supposed to be used for our food?" By thinking of the possible consequences that you will experience when you give in to your urge to gamble, you will be further convinced that it is a behavior that you should never engage in.

Keeping yourself occupied

Similar to applying the daily scheduled activity, it is important that you continue to keep yourself busy even if there is no one to monitor you. If your mind is distracted with other activities, it will not bother to think of the insignificant tasks such as gambling. Substituting gambling with more productive activities such as going to the gym or attending chores at home will be a better use of your time than wasting money on gambling.

Keep postponing your gambling activities

If the urge to gamble is too strong, another method that may be used to suppress it is to continuously postpone the time that you'll be gambling. For example, you remind yourself that you will start with the activity after 10 minutes. If the urge to gamble is still strong after that, add another time interval.

Continue to engage in this "delay" until you lose interest in gambling or until you find other thing to do. Since we mentioned that the urge to gamble arises when there is idle time, you need to make sure that gambling has no opportunity to encroach in your life again – its either you keep yourself busy or you consciously block your thoughts to gamble until it can be resisted. As you get used to blocking your thoughts and not giving in on your urges, the thought of even gambling will eventually stop.

Connect with significant people in your life

Some people see gambling as a way to get connected with other people, whether in real-life casinos or in virtual ones. As mentioned in the previous chapter, gambling addicts sometimes find their relationships dysfunctional. This influences them to seek more functional relationships such as gambling venues, where they can hang out with people who understand them and in turn build social networks with them.

However, there are many ways on how they can substitute their "gambling buddies" with healthier relationships. Reconnecting with friends, their partner and their children is far better than building social networks elsewhere. They may also improve their relationships with other groups of people such as work colleagues or schoolmates.

These people may also help you if you manage to get in touch with them the moment that you have a strong urge to gamble and that you're experiencing difficulties in suppressing it. They will encourage you to stay away from gambling with their words or prevent you from exhibiting the behavior with their actions (such as taking another route when planning to go out to avoid any casinos along the way, or removing possible triggers for your gambling).

Self-exclusion

There are instances when the person who has finished therapy and became independent from gambling can still feel the urge to gamble, especially if he has access to anything that might tempt him to do it (such as getting past a casino). A way to help him further avoid going back to these places is to "self-exclude".

This practice is similar to getting "blacklisted" in that they will not be allowed to gamble in that specific casino. By doing so, they won't have a chance to go back to their former state. Although the individual can choose to lie about his identity or disguise in order to gamble, self-exclusion is still a good method. This is because any gambler who wins a large amount of money is required to fill out papers for proper tax filing (since prize winnings are taxable).

If the gambler who is supposed to be there wins the jackpot or any large amount of money, then his identity will be revealed. Since he should not be there in the first place, the casino will then refuse to give him the prize. Without the chance of winning a large prize, most gamblers will not even be enticed to gamble.

Self-exclusion on gambling websites, however, is not possible. One solution that you can apply is to make sure that every possible gambling website is blocked on your computer.

Undergoing financial counseling

Aside from being involved in psychological counseling, the gambling addict can also utilize the help of financial counselors in order to cure his addiction. These financial professionals provide the following services:

- Financial counselors use figures to encourage them to stop gambling. Aside from their words, financial counselors use actual figures such as presentation of cash flow or balance sheets to make gamblers see how gambling is greatly affecting their financial status.

- They can provide feasible solutions to help the individual get back on track. Along with the presentation of the gambler's financial status, these counselors also provide them with practical tips that can be used to improve their finances. This includes analysis of the person's expenses and income and how it can be used to pay back what the gambler lost without compromising the family's needs.

By helping the gambler get through his financial crisis without actually shelling out money or paying for his debts, he will become more responsible in managing his finances as well as stop gambling – the source of the financial crisis in the first place.

Stay away from easy money

Money is a huge trigger that influences those who have finished their therapy sessions to continue gambling or re-develop the undesirable behavior. Aside from its promise to give a huge payout to those who placed a bet and won, having easy access to money (both actual money and credit cards) that can be used for gambling can also trigger them to bet. Thus, if the gambler does not have access to sufficient funds, they might find it difficult to continue with the activity.

With this in mind, there is a need to prevent the gambler from getting easy access to money. Some possible solutions for this include automatic payments/deductions from the bank to the agency where money should be paid, changing PINs or even getting rid of credit cards, having a savings account that requires two signatures before withdrawals can be made and carrying an amount of money that is just enough to get through the day. Remember, gambling addicts will never back out on a bet as long as they have enough funds – this is something that should be prevented.

Getting rid of gambling addiction requires the effort of both the therapist, as well as the affected individual. By applying the steps mentioned, they can control their urge to gamble without assistance from the therapist. It's just a matter of time before they will be able to resist the urge completely and even prevent any thoughts of gambling from recurring.

4: Utilizing the Bond to Pull Them Out Of Gambling Addiction

The family members of an addicted individual, especially his spouse, may be the best non-professional who may provide assistance from his gambling addiction. Since they are the first to experience the effects of gambling addiction in the family, they may be the first ones who can help them with this addiction

This chapter will outline some of the Do's and Don'ts that should be observed by the husbands and wives of gambling addicts.

What the spouse should do

Here are some of the things that the spouse should do to support their partners:

- Be the first to explain to your children about the situation. As the spouse, you need to make sure that your children understand the situation that their father or mother is going through. This is done so that the negative evaluations and attitudes of the other parent will not be developed. Because if it does, it may result into further conflicts within the family. The spouse of the affected individual should become the mediator between the other parent and the children.

- Be in charge of your finances. Since gambling involves money, it is also necessary that you oversee the family's financial status (if the gambling addict has been doing this prior to his condition). You need to review the family's cash flow, as well as monitor credit card or bank statements. This is to ensure that no one will be compromising their needs despite the presence of the gambling problem.

  It is also the first step to ensure that the family's financial situation doesn't get worse. By controlling the finances, you are also able to control how much your husband/wife will gamble.

- Consider getting professional help as early as possible. Gambling addiction is a psychological problem in nature. Even if the problem has just started, it would be best if you seek the help of mental health experts as soon as possible. The fact that the person is addicted simply means that the problem has been present and unattended for quite some time. By seeking help from a professional, treatment can be applied before their addiction gets worse.

- Speak calmly about the problem. It was mentioned that the affected individual engages in gambling because he finds the relationship as dysfunctional. If this is the case, then the spouse should resort to discussing the situation with the partner in a calm and reasonable manner. This creates an accepting atmosphere between the couple, making the addict comfortable of sharing his/her feelings or insights about the situation.

  The spouse should also discuss the consequences of gambling while remaining calm. This will show the addicted partner that his spouse has genuine concern over him and is non-judgmental, which may lead to changes (since the relationship became more functional).

What the spouse shouldn't do

If you, as the spouse, want to help and support your partner to get through this problem, then the following should be avoided:

- Lecture your partner or easily get angry. If you continue to lecture your partner or lose your temper and get influenced by your anger, then the relationship will become more dysfunctional. Worse, it may further influence your partner to continue gambling so as to get over the problems within the family. Although being in a situation that can ruin your relationship and jeopardize your financial status is provoking, you still need to be the source of calmness in an already chaotic setting.

- Deny that any problem exists. Some spouses are ashamed that other people will know about the difficulty experienced by their partners to the point that they need to consult a professional to help them get over it. This results to lying and thinking that the situation is manageable without help.

This may also lead to denying the existence of the problem. However, both these actions will never help your partner to recover from gambling addiction. It is only by admitting that your addicted partner needs help that he can receive one from those who are capable of giving it.

- Expecting that recovery from the condition is immediately experienced. The effectiveness of therapy varies across individuals. Even the greatest therapists cannot cure the gambling addict immediately, regardless of how severe the condition is.

As mentioned on the previous sections, cooperation from the patient is necessary for the therapy to produce its promised results. Aside from that, the spouse should not expect all problems will end if his/her partner stops gambling. You have to remember that any form of addiction has a high chance of recurrence, especially if the urges are not suppressed or if triggers are not removed.

Spouses are in the best position to help their husbands/wives who are struggling because of their gambling behavior. After all, they are the only ones who are able to get close to their partner. Making use of this distance to influence them into changing for the better is another good method to get rid of gambling addiction aside from psychotherapy and self-help.

With the observance of the Do's and avoidance of the Don'ts in this chapter, it will be easier for the addicted individual to get support and immediately overcome the behavior with the support and guidance of his spouse.

5: Biblical Reasons Why Gambling Is Wrong

1. Covetousness

What motivates a person to gamble? When I think about why people gamble, two things come to my mind - greed and covetousness. One of the Ten Commandments in the Bible states, "Thou shall not covet." Now the definition of covet on dicitionary.com is "To lust after, long for, or desire something that belongs to someone else."

Exodus 20:17 - You shall not covet your neighbor's house; you shall not covet your neighbor's wife, nor his male servant, nor his female servant, nor his donkey, nor anything that is your neighbor's. But what about the neighbor's money that is on the table? How do you sit around the table and gamble over a poker game and not violate this passage?

In Luke 12:15, Jesus said, "Take heed and beware of covetousness, for one's life does not consist of abundance of things he possesses." Now why is gambling wrong? Because of what it motivates men to do.

2. Gambling preys on the weaknesses of others. Gambling is recession-proof and is addictive.

Christian principles are just the opposite of this. Galatians 6:10 - Christian principles teach us, as we have the opportunity; let us do good to all men. Now, that would involve helping those who are in need, not taking their money!

3. Christian principles teach us to help the poor, to feed the hungry. But gambling does the opposite: it steals from the poor, and it robs the hungry. You know, it disturbs me to hear that the busiest day in the Atlantic City casinos is the day after the welfare checks are sent out. That means the people who can't afford to gamble are in the casinos hoping to strike it rich!

A gambler may win at the loss of one who can least afford it - it preys on the weaknesses of others. It profits from the pain of others.

A disproportionate number of people who play the lottery are very poor, and they take food away from children's mouths hoping to win the lottery. Study has found that the poor bet approximately three times the amount wagered by the person in the middle and upper income areas.

4. The "fruit test" – Matthew 7:15-20

Jesus laid down the principles, a test by which every activity, every philosophy could be measured. He said,

"Every good tree bears good fruit, but a bad tree bears bad fruit." A good tree cannot bear bad fruit, nor can a bad tree bear good fruit. Now let's ask ourselves, what kind of fruit does gambling produce?

When legalized gambling arrives in a new community, does it raise the moral standards of that community? Does it help the hardship of others and the less fortunate, or is it just the opposite? Gambling doesn't pass the fruit test!

Eight months after a casino opened in Gulfport, Mississippi, Gulfport police department noted the following:

- Murder increased by 75%

- Rape increased by 200%

- Robbery increased by 300%

- assaults increased by 64%

- Burglary increased by 100%

- Car theft increased by 160%

Here is another sad statistic from the great state of Nevada:

- 1st in suicide

- 1st in divorce

- 1st in homicide against women

- 1st in people with gambling addiction

5. Proverbs 13:11 English Standard Version

"Wealth gained hastily will dwindle, but whoever gathers little by little will increase it." Hastily we all know means fast - such as fast money, which also can be related to gambling.

Conclusion

I hope this book was able to help you to prevent and get rid of gambling addiction for life. It is difficult to cure or manage gambling addiction by using only one method. Recovering from the addiction requires the combined efforts of the loved ones of the addicted individual, professionals who has knowledge in dealing with this condition and the sufferer himself.

This book covers the things that you need to do to break the cycles of gambling addiction. Getting addicted to gambling is a bad habit that you need to cut off as early as possible. If you do not do something to break this habit, then you will end up breaking your relationship with your family, friends and other people who are close to you.

Gambling is just like any other addiction such as drugs and alcohol. Although gambling can offer some form of entertainment, most likely it will give you additional stress and you will feel worse than before with devastating financial losses.

With the help of the tips presented in this book, the road to recovery can start right away. You can break free from the addiction and live a normal, happier and more satisfying life.

By applying the knowledge imparted by this book into your daily habits and lifestyle, getting rid of your own or your loved one's gambling addiction for life is truly possible.

CPSIA information can be obtained at www.ICGtesting.com
Printed in the USA
BVOW11s1814280515

402288BV00010B/67/P